Tax Loopholes

For Everyone

Stefan Bernstein

The author is a qualified tax consultant with practices in London and Wiltshire. He advises corporations and individuals on their financial planning strategies. In addition, he is a registered representative of the Stock Exchange and a founder member of the Institute of Financial Planning.

HILITE
PUBLISHING

Take That Ltd.
P.O.Box 200
Harrogate
HG1 2YR
Fax:01423-526035
sales@takethat.co.uk

You should take independent financial advice before acting on material contained in this book

Printed and bound in Great Britain

ISBN 1-873668-64-3

Contents

Appendices

ACKNOWLEDGEMENTS

My dear Pieski has always been a beacon in the sometimes murky nights that can so often stretch before a tortured mind.

For advice on presentational matters, considerable thanks is due to Mrs Madeleine England, without whom the preparation of this book would have been almost impossible.

I would also like to thank my many friends who have always been generous in their support and encouragement throughout my writing career.

Finally, a special vote of thanks to Headline P.R. and Marketing whose understanding of the nuances of meaning in the English language, and further, less tangible aspects of communication has been invaluable to me.

Stefan Bernstein, 1998

Introduction

£ This book will tell you how to increase your net income through proper tax planning. It will give you the same "inside track" used by the very wealthy, the pop stars, the rich and the famous. This is normally only available either through bitter experience or by paying vast fees to accountants and lawyers. But now the secrets are open to anyone with the time and interest to read this book.

One thing to make clear from the start is that we are not talking about pennies and pounds. We are talking about hundreds, thousands and tens of thousands of pounds that may be saved by using knowledge which is now easily available to everyone. Thousands of pounds in your bank account and not the Exchequer's.

As well as actual loopholes, such as areas where the taxman may have left the door open through drafting the law incompletely, we also concentrate on getting you all your entitlements and making sure that the system works for you and not against you. Even outside of what may be considered loopholes, there are a great many opportunities for you to reduce the burden of taxation on your capital and income. Remember, if you pay less tax, you should have more to spend, more net income in your pocket, and you will increase your wealth base far more quickly as a result.

So, in this book you will find information on loopholes for the individual; covering Income Tax, National Insurance, Capital Gains Tax and Inheritance Tax.

The book is structured to give you all the facts and figures you need with worked examples. There are also sections on the law and how to use the tax system to your advantage. Finally, there are case studies based on two families with different approaches to their finances, and a large number of worked examples to amplify the text.

But before all this, and to whet your appetite, we begin with the real big money loopholes in section one.

Tax Avoidance & Tax Evasion
- An Important Note

Neither the authors nor the publishers can accept any liability whatsoever for the ideas contained in this book. Our advice to you is that if you have identified which loopholes apply to you and consider there to be considerable amounts of tax at stake, then you should engage a properly qualified professional adviser. Most reasonable accountants and tax consultants will certainly see you for one exploratory meeting at no cost. They should quickly be able to identify the amount of tax which you might save and you can then estimate whether or not their fees in this regard represent value for money.

If you do decide to go it alone, then you really must understand the crucial difference between tax avoidance and tax evasion.

Tax avoidance is what this book is all about. It is a well established principle that you can manage your affairs to legitimately reduce your tax burden. So, for example, you can transfer assets between yourself and your spouse, you can redirect your entitlement under a will and you can claim against tax the cost of the petrol you use legitimately in your business. On a more sophisticated level you might put together an offshore bond scheme within a discretionary trust. But the point is this - all the strategies are entirely legitimate. The fact that they advantage you and disadvantage the Exchequer is irrelevant.

Tax evasion is a different matter. This is a process whereby you avoid the burden of taxation through illegitimate means, for example, not declaring your bank account interest. This is illegal, and the penalties are stiff, as several celebrities have discovered in recent years.

Given that so many thousands of pounds may be saved legitimately through proper tax planning, there is no need to be involved in tax evasion, and the authors and publishers state here unequivocally that this book is in no way intended to encourage any reader to break the law. It just isn't necessary.

Now read on, and discover what you can, quite legitimately, do to put very significant sums in your pocket.

The Really Big Money Loopholes

General

£ Whilst it is important to make sure your affairs are in order, that you have got your allowances, that you are using the taxman as a bank, and all the other ideas in this book, it is the big glamorous loopholes that are likely to save you the most money.

This section sets out 10 areas of enormous opportunity for the bold. Some of these schemes are well documented and well known to the Revenue. Some involve no contentious issues at all. Nonetheless, some do, and we remind you that we take no responsibility for these schemes, nor any credit for *the tremendous amounts of money that can be saved.*

The Offshore Roll-Up Fund

T housands of people in the U.K. could benefit immediately from this idea. Anyone with building society deposits can avoid tax altogether on the interest, saving hundreds or thousands of pounds over a few years.

Instead of having the interest on your capital taxed as it is credited, and then paid to you or accumulated net of tax, you may accumulate it offshore in a roll-up fund without paying any tax at all. The first benefit of this is that the account will grow much faster because of compound interest. The second is that by timing your receipt of the funds, you may effectively retain them within your overall affairs, completely tax free. The table below demonstrates how on reasonable assumptions the compounding effect over the years becomes greater and greater.

Assume gross rate of interest 10%, 7.7% net of 23% tax.

End of Year	£ Onshore	£ Offshore roll-up
1	10,770	11,000
2	11,599	12,100
3	12,492	13,310
4	13,454	14,641
5	14,490	16,105
6	15,606	17,716
7	16,808	19,487
8	18,101	21,436
9	19,496	23,579
10	20,997	25,937

Tax due on roll-up fund say £15,937 x 23% = £3,665

Net onshore fund	£20,997
Net offshore fund	£22,272
Gain Tax free	£ 1,275

Imagine that in the year the funds are repatriated, you use your excess gain to invest in a pension scheme. The example below demonstrates how your wealth will be greater by employing this strategy.

Tax free gain	£1,275	
Rolled into a pension	£1,656	(23% tax payer)
	£2,125	(higher rate payer)

So by the simple measure of controlling the 'tax point' on your investment you can be thousands of pounds ahead.

Tax Relief on Mortgage Capital

Most of us are familiar with the availability of tax relief on mortgage interest. We get it automatically through the M.I.R.A.S. system and it's worth about £240 a year to most people. But now it is being phased out so you will need to be far cleverer in your approach to your mortgage. For example, by structuring a pension mortgage you can actually get tax relief on the capital itself, which will be far more valuable.

Imagine that you have a mortgage of £30,000 and the gross interest is 10% p.a. If you have an endowment mortgage, you will pay the interest on the loan net of interest relief, namely 8.5%, and you will pay into the endowment policy from your net income.

However, if you support your mortgage with a pension policy, then not only will you get tax relief on the interest you pay on the capital as above, but you will also get tax relief on the capital you build up through the pension.

The example below demonstrates the difference.

	£	£
Interest payment to lender (net) p.a.	2,550	2,550
Endowment premium (say)	500	
Net pension premium (relating to tax free cash, i.e. 1/4 of total)		225
Annual cost	3,050	2,775
Proceeds of Endowment policy	£30,000	
Tax free cash from pension	£30,000	

A 40% taxpayer could make over £1,000 a year every year by this method.

How To Get Tax Relief
For Your Income
of Seven Years Ago

There are generous rules concerning tax relief on personal pensions and retirement annuity policies (older style pensions). These may be combined to form a massive loophole which can leave you paying no tax at all in a particular year, and effectively getting tax relief from the late 1980's with all the appropriate interest repayments from the taxman.

Basically, there are three rules which need to be combined. The one allows you to deem any personal pension payment made in one year of assessment, to be treated as if it were made in the previous year. So if you make a payment in 1998/99, you can have it treated as though you had paid it in 1997/98, even though you didn't.

The other rule concerns the carry forward of your pension relief. What this says is that if you run out of relief in a particular year, you can then take up relief you didn't use for the six preceding financial years. If you combine this with the election to carry back, detailed above, then you will see that eight years of assessments may be involved.

Thus, in the 1998/99 tax year, you may make a payment that can be deemed to have been made in 1997/98 and take up relief from 1991/92 onwards. The example below shows how this works.

A self-employed individual aged 30 had the following earnings but made no previous pension provision.

		Maximum Pension relief
	£	£
1990/91	10,000	1,750
1991/92	12,000	2,100
1992/93	13,000	2,275
1993/94	14,000	2,450
1994/95	15,000	2,625
1995/96	17,000	2,975
1996/97	18,000	3,150
1997/98	19,000	3,325

In 1998/99, the individual may make a payment of £18,910 made up as follows:

		£
Relief for	97-98	3,325
	96-97	3,150
	95-96	2,975
	94-95	2,625
	93-94	2,450
	92-93	2,275
	91-92	2,100

Should he not make the carry back election he will lose the 91/92 relief for ever and his maximum payment will be £16,800.

If he pays only £15,000 but makes the election, he will be left with £750 of excess relief for 1995/96 and 3,150 for 1996/97 to be carried forward for up to six financial years. Effectively he will receive a tax rebate of over £7,000, more than he will actually pay in the current year!

Immediate Vesting Pensions

Many people think pensions are long term, but if you are old enough you can invest in a pension one day and take out the proceeds the next!

The example below shows how you can lock in to a return of 15.9% to 23.5% per year for the rest of your life as long as you know how to exploit the rules properly. If you combine this strategy with the carry back election and the carry forward of relief, the results can be dramatic.

This shows how it is done.

	23% Tax Payer £	40% Tax Payer £
Amount invested in Pension	10,000	10,000
Net cost (say)	7,700	6,000
Less tax free cash (taken the next day)	(2,500)	(2,500)
Actual net outlay	5,200	3,500
Pension for life (11% annuity rate)	825 p.a.	825 p.a.
Equivalent percentage rate	15.9%	23.5%

So instead of leaving all your money in the bank and worrying about interest rates, lock in to double figures for ever.

Avoiding The Earnings Cap

When the 1989 Budget was passed, the sneaky provision that many people missed was the imposition of a cap on earnings for the purposes of pension relief. What this means is that the government has set a level of earnings above which pension relief will not apply. So all the facilities mentioned previously will not be available for relief exceeding the earnings cap.

When this cap came in, it was based on £60,000 of earnings and so did not affect very many people. However, it is linked only to the RPI and not to National Average Earnings, which rise faster. So as each year goes by the effective level of the cap is reduced so that within 10 or 20 years, millions more people will be caught in the trap whereby they cannot make sufficient pension provision.

The example below uses big figures because that is the current situation, but it is easy to imagine a time when £84,000 is a national average wage because of years of inflation.

Current Pensions Cap   £84,000

Equivalent if individuals earnings rise faster than the cap.

	5 Yrs	10 Yrs	15 Yrs	20 Yrs
3%	70,755	61,250	52,613	54,103
5%	65,830	60,019	39,459	30,972
7%	58,542	41,726	29,737	21,208

As you can see, the cap will have shrunk to only £21,000 in 20 years time if average earnings rise at a rate 7% greater than the RPI.

So, how do you avoid it?

Well, the key is that the cap only applies to personal pensions andnot to old style retirement annuity contracts. The trouble is, old style retirement annuity contracts were less flexible as to retirement date so that you have to wait until you are 60 at the earliest, whereas personal pensions let you retire at 50.

The loophole is this - make all your payments through your old retirement annuity schemes, avoiding the cap and having effectively almost unlimited payments. Then, when you are ready, transfer from your retirement annuity schemes to your personal pension and retire at 50. You have got round the cap, and you have retired at 50 as though the cap had never existed.

You will need to ask your pension company what type of scheme you have and then take advice from a qualified consultant, but for people with fluctuating earnings or profits, the amount of money saved could run into the thousands.

Independent Taxation

The money to be saved from independent taxation planning can be enormous. Married couples can be thousands of pounds better off. By ensuring that the assets are in the right hands at any one time, you will guarantee that you receive the maximum tax allowance and the maximum amounts of tax free income and gains.

The example below shows how much you can increase your income, but this doesn't simply apply to income tax. For example, imagine you have a shareholding worth £20,000 that has cost only £5,000. If it is owned by only one spouse, then the tax payable is likely to be a minimum of £2,250.

However, by ensuring that the holding is split between husband and wife before sale, the tax can be reduced to £750, by using two annual capital gains exemptions. A saving of £1,500. Thousands of pounds can be saved in both income and capital taxes, as in the example below.

John and Mary Smith have the following assets.

	£	
House	50,000	(net of mortgage)
Shares	10,000	
Building Society	20,000	

John earns £31,500 a year and Mary £1,000 part-time.

The shares and cash bring in £2,500 gross and are currently owned in John's name.

Their total tax is as follows:

	John	Mary	
	£	£	
Income (earned)	31,500	1,000	
Income (investment)	2,500		
TOTAL	34,000	1,000	
Personal relief (say)	(5,500)	(1,000)	
Taxable	28,500	NIL	
20% 4,000	(860)		
23% 22,800	(5,244)		
40% 1,700	(680)		
TOTAL net income	27,216	1,000	28,216
TOTAL tax			6,784

However, if John and Mary now transfer the shares and cash into Mary's name, the savings will be almost £1,000 per year.

	£	£	
Income (earned)	31,500	1,000	
Income (investment)		2,500	
TOTAL	31,500	3,500	
Personal relief (say)	(5,500)	(3,525)	
Taxable	26,000	Nil	
20% 4,000	(860)		
23% 22,000	(5,244)		
40%	NIL		
TOTAL net income	25,396	3,500	28,896
TOTAL Tax			6,104
		TAX SAVED	**£680**

How To Change Somebody's Will After They're Dead

You might think that your will would be followed to the letter once you're dead. But you'd be wrong. You can beat the tax-man from the grave. Imagine that a chap dies with an estate of £400,000 and leaves it to his wife. Out of complete shock, she dies the next day and his estate is added to hers of a further, let's say, £150,000, so that the whole £550,000 passes to their children. In this case, £327,000 will be chargeable at 40%, with a huge tax bill of over £130,000.

However, by using a "Deed of Variation" it is possible to re-write the man's will, so that £223,000 of his estate (the current nil rate band), passes to the beneficiaries on his death. This means that the wife's taxable estate would now be only £327,000, with a resulting tax bill of only £41,600, and a saving in tax of £88,400.

As long as all parties to the will agree, and they would be foolish not to, the will may be re-drawn in almost any fashion. Legacies may be redirected, the order of gifts changed, and masses of tax saved.

Self Managed Pension Schemes

This one allows you to play the investment markets, make as much as you can and never pay one penny of tax on the gains. Imagine you inherit £20,000 and decide to play the Stockmarket. You manage to double your money three times in 10 years and then sell all your holdings.

Not only will you have paid tax on the dividends throughout, but you will have paid capital gains tax on the disposals you have made. Moreover, you will have begun by playing with "net money".

By structuring this through a self-managed pension, you would get the following benefits.

●   All dividends would be free of tax.

●   All the growth you make will be free of capital gains tax.

●   Because of the operation of tax relief going in to the pension, you will not need to risk as much of your capital, or alternatively, can make bigger gains. The example below demonstrates this.

	Personal Holding £	Self invested Pension £
Initial capital	20,000	26,000 (1)
10 Yr picture (dividends reinvested, CGT on 'doubling')	122,000	218,000 (2)
Improvement	£96,000	

Notes: (1) Pension net of initial charges, grossed up.

(2) Dividends constant at £1,000 gross p.a.

Year by year you can build up a bigger and bigger tax free pot. And as people generally build up such nest eggs for retirement, it is quite possible to take a tax free lump sum at 50 and live off the income for the rest of your life.

Exploiting Age Allowance

Next time granny is moaning about the weather, tell her about the tax she can save by using Age Allowance. People over 65, or over 74 can qualify for extra income tax allowances of £1,215 and £1,405 respectively. However, these allowances are clawed back if your income exceeds a certain level. What matters here is the definition of "income".

Some forms of income are not taxable, such as the basic 5% annual withdrawals from investment bonds, a stream of capital receipts, the income up to £70 from National Savings Bank ordinary accounts, and many of the other items discussed in the text.

So by carefully structuring your income so that you have a high proportion of such holdings, you can ensure that your net spendable income, which is always what matters, is as high as possible. The example below illustrates this.

A 78 year old single taxpayer wishing to increase net income.

Before reorganisation	£	
Total income	17,500	
Maximum level	(16,200)	
	1,300 x 50% = £650	
		restriction
Total income	17,500	
Personal allowance		
i.e. (5,410 - 650) = 4,760	(4,760)	
Taxable income	12,740	
20% on 4,300	(860)	
23% on 8,440	(1,941)	
Net income	14,699	

After reorganisation

	£
Total income	16,700
Maximum	(16,200)
	500 x 50% = £250
	restriction
Total income	16,700
Personal allowance	
i.e. (5,410 - 250) = 5,160	(5,160)
Taxable income	11,540
20% on 4,300	(860)
23% on 7,240	(1,665)
Net income	14,175
Plus non-taxable	800 (1)
Total net income	14,975
SAVING	£276

NOTES: (1) Assuming money moved from bank to N.S. ordinary account and to on-shore investment bond.

Income Tax

General

Before undertaking any income tax planning, try to remember one important fact - it is not how much tax you save, it is the net return to you that matters. The intellectual buzz may be nice, beating the taxman may be nice, but success is usually defined as pounds in your pocket. If a scheme gives you a tax free income of 5%, but you can get a gross income of 10% and pay tax on it, you will normally be better off paying tax. Don't let the tail wag the dog and always look at the net return to you, what you have left over to spend.

What's Tax Free

Having said that the first place to start on income tax planning is to look at what's tax free and make sure you benefit from it as fully as possible. Thankfully, there are loads of thingswhich are tax free, in fact there are so many receipts that are not liable for tax that you should try to arrange to receive as many of them as practically possible, always bearing in mind the net return.

The list below gives an idea of some tax free receipts.

- Your first £70 of interest from National Savings Bank ordinary deposits. This means £140 in total for husband and wife.

- The capital element of a Purchased Life Annuity-Unlimited.

- Interest on certain National Savings Certificates.

- Premium Bond winnings and Lottery prizes.

- The profits from casual gambling such as horse racing or the football pools.

- Tax free lump sums from pensions and redundancy payments.

- Several Social Security benefits such as Child Benefit, Family Income Supplement and Sickness Benefit.

- Profit Related Pay.

By simply ensuring that you receive your entitlements, you can put thousands of pounds into your pocket.

Getting Your Allowances

One of the best ways of minimising tax is to ensure that you have properly claimed your allowances. For example, any widow in the year of her husband's death and the following year, as long as she has not remarried, is entitled to widow's bereavement allowance, currently £1,900 p.a. of tax allowance. Over two years this could save £570 of tax! Over £20 per month to help at a very difficult time.

There is also an additional personal relief, also worth £1,900 p.a. of tax free allowance, for widows, widowers or single parents, who are not entitled to the married couples allowance but who have minor children resident with them. This includes properly legally adopted children and stepchildren. As long as a child is under 16 at the beginning of the tax year, or a full time student at school or university, the relief should be available. Once again, get on the phone to the taxman and then drop him a line claiming the allowance if appropriate.

Age Allowance

You can actually benefit by being old. If you are a granny, you can boost your income and if you've got a granny, she can give you the extra!

If you are over 65 by the beginning of the tax year, you are entitled to an extra personal allowance, and if you are over 74, an even bigger one. This allowance however, is taken away if your income exceeds £16,200 p.a. So, if your income is round about this figure, you will need to take steps to exploit the loophole and obtain the allowance. Section one demonstrates how this allowance may be obtained by a simple rejigging of your affairs.

Children's Income

There's a lot to be gained by using your children and their tax allowances. The general rule is that if you give capital to your children, then the income arising from it will be assessed back on you. Otherwise, everybody could give their children some £50,000 (at current rates) and it could be held almost tax free in a bank or Building Society.

However, when the funds come from a third party, such as grandparents, then any income arising from that capital is deemed to belong to the children, and may therefore be tax free by exploiting the children's personal allowances. Each child may receive £4,195 of income per annum without paying tax. So, you can save £1,678 per child in the family unit, or £965 if you pay 23% tax.

It is common for grandparents to give money to their grandchildren. It is also common for the middle generation to be giving money to, or taking money from, their parents. In this case, it could be that the middle generation give money to their parents who then give it on to the children.

This of course would not be correct from the point of view of the tax authorities, although it would be very difficult to discover which money belonged to which party when families are involved. The rule here is to be very careful, and make sure you don't break the law.

Overseas Income

It is not always possible to avoid tax completely on overseas income, but at least you have the opportunity to decide when you pay it. For example, with capital in a UK bank account, the interest simply arises and is taxed, probably at source. By using an offshore roll-up fund, not only will the interest roll-up gross and therefore interest will compound on interest, but you may choose when you pay the tax by timing the repatriation of the funds.

For example, if you are a 40% tax payer, you may choose to bring the funds back to the UK at a time when your income is low, perhaps due to business losses, Lloyds losses, (taking advantage of the bad times) or Pension payments, so that you only pay tax at a lower rate than you would have during the holding of the account. Section 1 takes this point further as it is one of the simplest and most attractive of loopholes.

Independent Taxation

For some years now the income of a husband and wife has been treated separately. This has led to massive tax planning opportunities and loopholes to be exploited. Section 1 gives a worked example of how thousands of pounds may be saved year after year after year. The basic principle is, that as far as is practical, a married couple should make sure that income arises in the hands of the individual less likely to pay tax on it, or less likely to pay tax at the higher rate. The maximum saving in this regard would save enough money to buy a classic Jaguar, a new kitchen or seventy five Harrods Hampers.

For example, imagine a husband and wife are both working and earning say £18,000 p.a. During one year, the wife may well stop work to start a family. At this point all the bank and Building Society accounts may be transferred into her name so that the income from them may be offset against her personal allowance and may be tax free. Once again, by careful planning, loopholes may be exploited, although you will need to be aware of the anti-avoidance rules, and tread carefully.

Interest On Overdue Tax

Now here is a way to treat the taxman as your banker. Deposit money with him and borrow it as it suits you. For example, if your tax payments are deemed to be overdue, then you will pay interest. However, interest can run from a variety of different dates, depending on when an assessment is raised.

Furthermore, if you appeal against the assessment and postpone the tax, you can buy yourself several extra months of interest free credit. You should box clever. For example, a quick telephone call to the Inland Revenue will establish what is the "official rate of interest".

This is not changed very frequently, unlike bank and Building Society interest and so, if you owe the taxman money and you are suffering a cashflow crisis, you are much better off owing the Revenue money at an official rate of interest which will always be far less than overdraft costs, both personal and business.

As long as you discover precisely when penalties may be levied and make sure you have paid by that date, you can get months of useful interest free credit from the tax man.

Conversely, if the taxman actually owes you money, and interest rates have been falling, then the official rate of interest may be higher than that available on instant access building society accounts. Moreover, the interest is tax free, so it would not be to your advantage to hound the taxman for a repayment.

By being on top of your affairs and understanding the system, you can effectively borrow at very low rates, or receive competitive tax free rates of interest depending on your position.

Fringe Benefits

There are a lot of benefits which you can extract from your employer without paying tax. For example, if your earnings are less than £8,500 p.a, including fringe benefits, and you are not a director of the company employing you, then a great many benefits may be tax free, including a company car. Also, such things as private medical care insurance may be tax free.

However, if you are a director or you earn more than £8,500 p.a. inclusive, you may well be taxed on fringe benefits, but generally you will still be ahead. (This was certainly the case with company cars for years, although it has been tightened up recently). For example, if you receive a private medical insurance benefit then you will be taxed on the cost to your employer.

If there are enough of you, you will get group rates from private medical insurance and will end up in front. For example, if the actual cost to you if you join BUPA personally is £500, then you will need to earn at least £667 to be left with £500 in your pocket with which to pay BUPA. However, if the group rate per head is say, £300, then the amount of tax you pay will only be £75 and so your BUPA is costing you only 1/9th of the true cost otherwise.

Appendix 1 gives a table of fringe benefits and their taxation for your reference.

Severance Payments

This is an area which the taxman has concentrated on over recent years, so the scope for exploiting the loophole has diminished. Nonetheless, the basic rule is that you can extract up to £30,000 tax free from your employer as long as it is a genuine ex-gratia payment.

Further, as long as this is not a contractual entitlement, i.e. written into your contract of employment, you will not pay tax. It would be very naughty indeed for an employee to arrange with his employer that certain payments to which he was entitled would be waived and paid as tax free redundancy.

Insurance Bonds

Insurance bonds are really single premium policies issued by Life Assurance companies. Because Life Assurance companies pay corporation tax on their income and gains, such bonds provide a "tax free" return to investors. What they are really doing is providing a return that is completely free of basic rate tax. In certain circumstances you can pay higher rate tax, (or, more accurately, the difference between the two).

If you take only 5% of the original capital invested as your annual income, then, irrespective of your tax position, you will not pay any more tax. However, the final day of reckoning will come when you either run out of 5% allowances (you are allowed 20 years of this), or decide to finally encash your policies.

In this case, a "chargeable event" happens. Here, the taxman compares the amount you invested with the profits you made and may well charge higher rate tax on the profit.

There are two ways in which you can exploit this. Firstly, you can buy such a bond when you are a higher rate payer and stay within your 5% annual limit. At some time in the future, when you encash it, you can time this encashment to fall in a year when, for some reason (large pension payments, business losses, lower income on retirement etc.) you are only a basic rate tax payer. In this way you would have avoided higher rate tax on the investment for the entire period of ownership, and the bond would have acted as a very useful shelter.

Another nice little wrinkle works on the "top slicing" method. What this means is that the taxman looks at the profit and then averages it over the entire period for which you have owned the investment. He then takes only the appropriate slice to determine whether or not you pay higher rate tax.

You can actually take out a policy with, say, £1,000, and then 10 years later add £100,000. The top slicing will work from the day of the original policy purchase, even though only £1,000 went in! These are known as "peg bonds" and should be more popular than they are because higher rate tax payers in particular can use them as tax-deferral mechanisms and save thousands of pounds by doing so.

Important Note. There are currently proposals to alter this tax treatment and it is thought that pre-existing schemes may be safe. So consider acting now if you have free capital.

Purchased Life Annuity

If you are old enough, and you should really be 65, you can buy a "purchased life annuity". This means you give an insurance company, say £10,000. They then gamble on your life expectancy and promise to pay you a level of income, say, £1,500 per annum, every year for the rest of your life. If you die before expected, you have lost out, but if you live a long time you can do very well.

What makes the annuity attractive is the tax treatment. The Inland Revenue have special tables which tell them how much of each £1,500 should be treated a return of capital and how much as income. They then only tax the income part.

So, imagine that on the example above only £300 is deemed to be income, then a 23% taxpayer would only pay a maximum of £69 tax. On the full £1,500 this works out at a tax rate of 4.6%.

Even more interesting is that, irrespective of age, you can get temporary annuities for a set number of years. Even with interest rates as low as 8%, a married couple in their 50's could lock into an effective net of tax return of 21%.

Accordingly, if they invest only one third of their capital in such a scheme, they would have a net return of 7% on the whole lot, and still have the other two thirds of their capital to grow. Just less than 9% net growth on that remaining capital would effectively mean they'd had their money back after the five year period. All this with no risk by simply accumulating one tax relief on another.

Section 3

National Insurance

£ Many people ignore National Insurance, but in effect it is an extra tax. Class 1 contributions for employees can be up to 10%, whilst employers can also pay 10%. Clearly this is a massive cost of employment and where it can be avoided quite legitimately, steps should be considered. After all, who wants to pay up to 50.0% tax on their income? Well, hundreds of company directors do just that!

For example, many of the fringe benefits referred to in Section 2 do not have a National Insurance levied on them. Moreover, some payments, such as Pension payments, may attract a liability to National Insurance if incorrectly structured. For example, imagine you are negotiating a new package with your employer and he offers to pay you more money so that you can fund a personal pension.

In this case, the employer will pay 10% National Insurance on the amount of money he gives you to put into the pension. If you simply arrange the pension so that the company makes the direct debiting payment and not you, then the 10% would be saved. Many employers will split this with you and thereby give you an extra five or so percent into your personal pension. There's usually a few hundred pounds to be shared out.

There are also several rather risky schemes where employers have paid bonuses or even basic salary in a form thought not to be liable to National Insurance. Here is how it works. Let's say there are 10 employees in a firm, each acting as a salesman earning £15,000 basic salary. They have a further £10,000 of bonus, and if the employer were to pay this as an ordinary PAYE salary, then £10,000 of National Insurance would be required on the

---

whole amount. However, he might pay the individuals by giving them Gold Shares or bullion itself. The individuals then sell the bullion and end up with the same amount of earnings they would have had they been paid normally, but the employer saves the National Insurance.

Such schemes need to be very carefully structured and the downside is that if they don't work, there will have been all the transaction costs on the buying and selling of the gold, along with the risk that whilst the bullion is held overnight by the employee, there could be a massive fall in the price. Nonetheless, many millions of pounds have been paid to employees on schemes such as this.

Clearly, the Exchequer is not keen on seeing all this revenue disappear and since the 1993 November budget, schemes which pay staff in the form of assets which can be traded on a recognised exchange are no longer effective. However, you may still be able to do this with assets which aren't readily tradeable, for example, fine wines. But, don't expect this loophole to remain open for long.

As you can see, National Insurance is not very easy to avoid. Exploit the fringe benefits position, and ensure your pension payments are structured correctly. Finally, if there is enough National Insurance at stake, take professional advice on an asset scheme or some of the other more obscure arrangements.

Capital Gains Tax

Introduction

£ A UK resident individual is basically taxable on any gains made in a year at the appropriate marginal tax rate of up to 40%. This means that if you buy a chargeable asset, such as British Telecom shares, and then sell at a profit, you'll be taxed on it. This includes gains made all over the world, so the sale of a Spanish property or any overseas shares will also count.

Each person is entitled to a £6,800 tax free allowance against their gains and this takes the sting out of most people's ordinary gains. However, the prospect of paying away 40% of your profit to the taxman is most unattractive so this section deals with means of legitimately avoiding that position.

What Is CGT-Free?

O nce again, there is a whole variety of items which are free from Capital Gains Tax. Areas where you can make tax-free profit. Certain items may not be much use, like betting winnings, including the football pools, or personal chattels (such as cars or furniture) sold for less than £6,000. However, the list below may provide some opportunities.

- ✔ Private cars.
- ✔ Your principal private residence, usually the house in which you live.
- ✔ Any foreign currency which is for your own use abroad.

- ✔ National Savings Certificates and Save as You Earn Schemes.

- ✔ British Government Gilts.

- ✔ Certain life assurance policies as long as you are the original owner.

- ✔ Business Expansion Scheme shares as long as you are the original owner and they were issued to you after 18th March 1986.

- ✔ Option Contracts in Gilts.

- ✔ Decorations for Valour, as long as you haven't bought them.

- ✔ Assets gifted to charity.

As you can see, there is less opportunity to arrange for the receipt of tax free capital gains above, and so you will need to understand the principles of the tax in order to arrange your tax affairs so as to avoid it.

How It Works

Basically, your sale proceeds, net of the costs of sale, are compared with the amount you paid for an asset, and the resulting gain, (after an inflation allowance), will be taxed at your ordinary rate of tax subject to your allowance of £6,000 being deducted.

It can get very complex if you owned the asset before March 1982 or April 1965 and separate calculations are necessary, you will probably require the services of an accountant or tax special-ist. Additionally, there are certain "pooling" rules for repeated purchases of the same shares over a given period. The example below sets out how a basic calculation might work.

	£
Sale proceeds of item	20,000
Cost of sale e.g. commission	(1,000)
Cost of item in June 1985	(6,000)
Gross gain	13,000
Indexation relief (see later)	(4,000)
Net gain	9,000
Personal exempt amount	(6,000)
Taxable gain	3,000
Tax at 23% or 40%	£690 or £1,200

Indexation Relief

In 1982, the Government recognised that a lot of the "profit" that people had made on their assets was really inflation. So they introduced a process known as "Indexation Relief", where they now seek to tax only the real gain made, having deducted the inflation allowance.

What basically happens is that the RPI for the month when the asset was acquired (or March 1982 if later) is compared with the RPI in the month when the asset is sold, or April 6 1998 if sooner.

This increase is then deducted from the profit so that only the true gain is left. However, a recent change in the law means that an allowance would not be available to increase or create an allowable loss.

Taper Relief

The 1998 Finance Act proposed a form of taper relief to replace Indexation. Here, relief would be given for having held on to assets for the long-term. There will be no relief unless an asset is held for a minimum of three years, so short-term speculators will be disadvantaged. The way to beat this one is to use an 'Umbrella Fund' or, if you are wealthy enough, a private unit trust. Here, all the gains on switching will be sheltered until you finally dispense of the overall fund, so that all your management decisions can be investment based and not tax based. This would also be true of a private managed pension fund (see page 18).

Losses And Gains

One loophole you must be aware of is the compulsory offset of losses and gains in any year of assessment. For example, imagine you make a gain of £6,000, you may be well pleased because your personal allowance covers this. (For sales after 6/4/98 you can choose which savings and losses to offset).

However, if in the same tax year you make a loss of, say, £3,000, then this will be offset against the gain first so that only the odd £3,000 is set against your personal allowance.

If you were to delay that loss until the following year, it would not be offset against this year's gains producing a much more useful loss for you. The example below shows how this might work.

Gain each year £5,000 and £10,000, loss of £3,000 in year one.

	£ Yr1	£ Yr2	£ Yr3	£ Yr4
Gain	5,000	10,000	5,000	10,000
Loss	(3,000)	NIL	NIL	NIL
Net Gain	2,000	10,000	5,000	10,000
Allowance	(6,800)	(6,800)	(6,800)	(6,800)
Taxable	NIL	3,200	NIL	3,200

If, however, the loss is deferred until year two, tax on £3,000 is saved.

	£ Yr1	£ Yr2	£ Yr3	£ Yr4
Gain	5,000	10,000	5,000	10,000
Loss	NIL	(3,000)	NIL	NIL
Net Gain	5,000	7,000	5,000	10,000
Allowance	(6,800)	(6,800)	(6,800)	(6,800)
Taxable	NIL	200	NIL	3,200

So, by delaying the sale of an asset, even by a little as one day, you could save between £690 and £1,200 in tax.

Bed And Breakfasting

Another timing issue for capital gains tax is that of "Bed and Breakfast" transactions. Here, the aim is to realise some of your gains each year in order to utilise some of your personal allowance, which would otherwise be wasted. This has been made much more difficult since the 1998 budget, but you can still take advantage.

Imagine a shareholding cost £5,000 several years ago and it is now worth £20,000. It is possible to "wash out" some of the gain by bed and breakfasting. What this means is that part of the asset is sold and immediately re-acquired. The idea behind this is that the sale will crystallise part of the gain, which can then be offset against your allowance. Not enough is sold to give you your tax liability.

The immediate re-acquisition will mean that the asset now has a higher starting cost for any future calculations. (Immediate is something of a misnomer, because there usually has to be an interval of a day between the two transactions.) The example below shows how this might work.

1. If sold now

	£
Sale proceeds	20,000
Cost	(5,000)
Indexation Relief	(2,000)
Gain	13,000
Exemption	(6,000)
Taxable	7,000
Tax at 23%	1,610

2. If part of holding is "bed and breakfasted"

	£
Sale Proceeds (say 40%)	8,000
Cost	(2,000)
Indexation relief	(800)
Gain	5,200
Exemption	(6,000)
Taxable	NIL

3. The following year, the entire holding is sold

	£
Sale Proceeds	20,000
Cost	(11,000)
Indexation relief	(1,300)
Gain	7,700
Exemption	(6,000)
Taxable	1,700
Tax at 23%	391
TAX SAVED	**1,219**

So, as you can see, there is a lot of money to be made through the "bed and breakfast" loophole.

The problem created by the proposals in the 1998 Finance Bill is that there are now special matching rules, so that if the share is re-acquired within 30 days, then the exercise is ignored ie. you will get no-where in terms of saving tax. So you have to stay out of the market for 30 days - which, if it is the stock market, could have disastrous consequences. There are several answers. One can change between similar stocks, for instance, selling Asda and buying Tesco. Or, if it is broadly based unit trusts, from one top manager to another. Of course, there is still some risk attached.

It also appears you can 'bed and spouse'. This means that you would sell the item in question and your spouse would re-aquire it. You will need to be extremely careful of the general anti-avoidance laws and the laws on settlements, but if you are really determined, you should be able to achieve your desired result.

The Family Home

For many people, the family home is a substantial asset, and if it has been owned for a reasonable period of time, it may stand at a considerable premium over its original cost. However, the good news is that your family home is generally completely free of capital gains tax on sale.

The problem arises however, for those people who have more than one house, perhaps as a result of a job move, a divorce or an inheritance. Here, careful planning is essential in order to avoid a tax charge on disposal of one or all of the properties.

During any period for which you have more than one house, you are supposed to make an election to the taxman to tell him which is your "principal private residence". In the absence of such an election, the taxman may choose for you. However, you have up to two years to decide which house to nominate and this may well give you a chance to see which way the property market is going. Moreover, you are allowed two years of tax free gain on the sale of a second house, so by carefully using the election, you can ensure the second house is tax free.

An example may help: Imagine your family home cost £50,000 ten years ago and is now worth £100,000. You have a second home that cost £20,000 five years ago and is now worth £50,000. If you say nothing and simply sell the second home, you will be liable for tax on around £30,000 subject to various reliefs.

However, you might wait until the end of year three and then make a retrospective election for the previous two years, that the second house is your main house. That will cover the gain for years two and three. Years four and five will be covered by the two year selling exemption, so now only one-fifth of the entire gain will be taxable and, with a bit of inflation relief, should fall within your annual exemption of £6,800.

The consequence is that you would effectively have produced two taxable years to your main home for the time during which it wasn't your actual main residence. However, this may well be washed out with indexation relief and your annual exemption on a later sale.

Selling Your Garden

One massive pitfall concerns selling your garden as a building plot. The law is generous and allows you a garden of up to one acre (half a hectare) with your family home. Beyond that size it is a question of what is suitable, bearing in mind the nature of

---

the property. So an 18th Century coaching house with stables and an orchard might get away with a garden of several acres. The issue is that the taxman wants to stop people having a little cottage and 50 acres and calling it a tax free garden.

But you must be extremely careful if you decide to sell off part of your garden as a building plot. Some people think they're clever and sell their house first and then the plot. If you do this, you will be taxable on the plot because it was no longer your garden. However, if you sell the plot first, you have, by definition, sold a part of your garden, and the gain should be tax free. With property development prices in the late 1980's, this could be a serious issue.

CGT And Death

You can save money by dying, as long as you are careful!

If you own assets which are liable to capital gains tax, then when you die, the whole gain is completely wiped out and your beneficiaries inherit those assets so that their own "original cost" for capital gains tax, will be the value at the date of your death. So, if someone in your family unit is a bit shaky healthwise, or very old, they should make gifts in their lifetime of non-chargeable assets before chargeable assets.

For example, imagine old Jack is 95 years old and very shaky, and decides to give £10,000 to his grandchildren. If he gives shares which cost him £1,000, then the gain will be realised by the gift and old Jack will face £9,000 of taxable gain. However, if he were to give them cash, and then let them inherit the shares when he died, the base cost they inherit would be £10,000 saving a potential tax bill of £2,250. You will need to be careful about interaction of CGT and inheritance tax. (See Section 5).

Further Timing Issues

Remember, capital gains tax is payable on December 1st in the tax year following that in which a disposal takes place. So imagine you sell your second home in November 1997, tax will be due on 1st December 1998.

So if you have any flexibility at all in making disposals, you might prefer not to make them at the end of a tax year, but at the beginning of the next.

For example, if you sell shares on April 4th 1998, the tax will be due on December 1st 1998. If the shares are sold on April 6th 1998, the tax will not be due until 1st December 2000, giving you use of the money for up to 20 months. If the tax is say, £10,000, then at 7% net interest, that's over £1,000!

Please bear in mind the points above on the use of exemptions, Bed and Breakfast, and other timing issues.

Gifts To Charity

Gifts to charity will normally be exempt from capital gains tax. So if you have £5,000 worth of privatisation shares that only cost you £2,000, and you have £5,000 in the bank, make sure you give the shares to the charity and not the cash.

The tax cost of doing it the wrong way round may be as much as £1,200, i.e. £3,000 x 40%. As you've saved £1,200 you can give that to the charity as well!

Enterprise Investment Schemes/Roll Over Schemes

Since the 1994 Finance Act schemes have become available which allow you to "roll-over" a capital gain instead of paying the tax. Broadly speaking, you must reinvest the gain you have made (not all the proceeds of the sale) into a qualifying company. At a stage in the future, the company will hope to create a market in the shares and you should be able to sell, gradually, perhaps each year within your annual exemption, and slowly take the gain out tax free. At the worst you will defer the tax.

You should be very careful however and ensure that you are not breaking a golden rule of investment. NEVER invest in a scheme just because of tax relief. Many early BES investors lost thousands by rushing into schemes on the back of 60% tax relief. That's no good if you lose all your money! So ensure first of all that the companies themselves are sound before investing a penny.

You can actually 'roll-over' capital gains into an Enterprise Investment Scheme, meaning a total of 60% tax relief is on offer. But, the same rules apply, make the investment only if you would have done anyway, and treat the tax relief as a bonus.

Inheritance Tax

General

£ Imagine the scene. You have paid tax all your life. Tax on your income, tax on your investments, you've paid capital gains tax, you've even paid VAT on most of the things you have bought. It has all become too much for you and you have decided to throw in the towel. But, there you are at the pearly gates, and who should be elbowing St. Peter out of the way? Yes, you've guessed it. Even when you die, some might say particularly when you die, the taxman is waiting.

Before you can even understand inheritance tax, you need to know what one or two important words mean.

"Domicile" is very important for inheritance tax. Generally speaking, you are domiciled in the country which you consider to be your natural home and where you intend to stay for the foreseeable future, or return to permanently at some time in the future. When you are born you acquire a "domicile of origin". This will usually follow on from that of your father at the time of your birth, irrespective of where you were actually born. Domicile can be changed but this is very difficult.

You can acquire a domicile of choice by living in a country and showing that you intend to live there permanently. This might mean for instance disposing of overseas property or making a UK will. Once you are domiciled in the UK then your world wide assets will be liable to inheritance tax. If you are not domiciled in the UK, then only your UK assets should be chargeable to inheritance tax.

But there is one further issue you should know about. This is the concept of "deemed domicile". What this means is that if you are in the UK for long enough, and look as though you might be acquiring a UK domicile, then you will be taxed as if you were UK domiciled and therefore the whole of your world wide estate will be included for inheritance tax. This can cost you a fortune, and if you are in any doubt about your status you should contact a competent professional advisor.

What Is Inheritance Tax?

Inheritance tax used to be known as capital transfer tax, and before that, death duties. The tax is based on the death value of your estate when it passes to people other than your spouse or a charity. The tax may also be levied on lifetime transfers, either immediately, or if you die within 7 years of such a transfer. If you are domiciled in the UK then your worldwide property will be liable to inheritance tax. If you are not UK domiciled then only your UK property will be liable.

How it works

	£
Value of Family Home	180,000
Mortgage	(20,000)
Shares and Peps	25,000
Building Society accounts and TESSAs	35,000
Chattels	25,000
Life Assurance policy claim values	60,000
TOTAL	305,000
Nil rate band	(223,000)
Taxable at 40%	82,000
Tax due	32,800
Net estate	272,200

The Nil Rate Band and Spouse Exemption

Personal allowances for inheritance tax are generous. You can leave or give £223,000 to any one individual. So for most people, inheritance tax will not be a problem. Moreover, there is a "spouse exemption", so that anything you give your husband or wife, either during lifetime or on death, is also free of inheritance tax. The problem will only arise when you are both dead.

The Seven Year Rule and Taper Relief

If you make a gift which is known as a PET (Potentially Exempt Transfer), as long as you live seven years, it will be completely free of tax. However, if you die in the seven year period, it will fall into charge with the rest of your chargeable estate. Fortunately, there is a taper relief. So if you die between years three and seven, the tax payable will be reduced in 20% increments down to zero. So it makes sense to make gifts as soon as you practically can in order to get the seven year clock running.

Gifts With Reservation

The taxman isn't stupid, and won't let you give things away but keep them. For example, if you have a collection of old masters on your walls, and you simply say to your children "right, this lot's yours", and leave them on your walls, the gift will not count. The old masters will still be part of your estate. The rule is that when you give something away, you must exclude yourself from benefitting. So it's no use passing over £50,000 into a Building Society account in your children's names, but having the cheque book and cash card for it. No, you need to be much smarter than that and you will be delighted to know that there are plenty of loopholes in this regard considered below.

Keeping The Value Outside The Estate

One of the main considerations is to keep your assets outside of your taxable estate. For example, you can have all your Life Assurance policies written in trust so that they do not form part of your taxable estate when you die, and simply pass straight to your chosen beneficiaries without any probate delay or inheritance tax. The example below shows how much tax might be saved, compared with the first example above.

	£
Value of Family Home	180,000
Mortgage	(20,000)
Shares and Peps	25,000
Building Society accounts and TESSAs	35,000
Chattels	25,000
TOTAL	245,000
Nil rate band	(223,000)
Taxable at 40%	22,000
Tax due	8,800
Net estate	236,200
Plus Insurance policies	60,000
Actual net estate	296,200
AMOUNT SAVED	**£24,000**

Use Your Reliefs

There are lots of gifts and transfers you can make each year which are not subject to inheritance tax. They are as follows:

✔ £3,000 Annual exemption. Each individual may give £3,000 away every year without any inheritance tax consequence at all. If you did not do this last year, then you may carry it forward and give away £6,000 this year. So a husband and wife can give £12,000 away, thus saving £4,800 in potential tax without any difficulty at all.

✔ £250 Gifts. Gifts of up to £250 may be given to anybody at all. They are unlimited and you could, theoretically, give £250 to every Millwall fan attending on a Saturday. However, curiously enough, if you give £251 to anybody, the whole £251 will be taxable and not just the odd £1!

✔ Gifts on Marriage. You are able to make gifts to one of the partners of a marriage or their children. The limits are £5,000 if the donor is a parent of one of the individuals getting married, or £2,500 if the donor is a grandparent or great-grandparent. Otherwise, e.g. Aunts and Uncles, the limit would be £1,000.

✔ Normal expenditure out of Income. You can give away almost any amount as long as it is seen to be a normal expenditure from your income, is not manifestly from capital, and is capable of being repeated year on year. So if you are retired with a fantastic index-linked pension of say, £50,000 p.a. and you only spend £10,000 a year, you could theoretically give the rest away as normal expenditure without inheritance tax consequences.

Skipping a Generation

This may appear to be mean, but it is actually very good planning.

Imagine that the grandparents have wealth they wish to dispose of. The natural inclination is to pass it on to their children. However, the children might well be middle aged and facing inheritance tax problems of their own. It just makes no sense to increase their estates. The grandparents should therefore consider giving the money directly to the grandchildren, (in trust if necessary), so that inheritance tax is never levied on that money in either their generation or the middle generation. (There are also important income tax benefits as discussed in Section 2.)

For example, imagine the grandparents leave £250,000 to the middle generation, and the tax is, say, £40,000. The net £210,000 seven years later may well have grown to £400,000. If the middle generation then die, then this might well be all taxed at 40% leaving a net amount of £240,000 for the grandchildren. Had the £210,000 gone directly to them, then all things being equal, they would now have the full £400,000 in their estate, so that £160,000 would be saved.

Properly Drafted Wills

Other than do-it-yourself dentistry, making your own will is probably the most stupid saving of a few quid you will ever make. Get a fixed quote from a solicitor and ensure the will is drafted properly.

For example, in the examples above, the family unit only ever benefits from £223,000 of nil rate band. However, by drafting the will properly you can benefit from two bites at this cherry.

For example, if John and Mary have a joint estate of £500,000 and each of their wills leaves everything to the other, they may find themselves with only one exemption. Imagine they are killed in a car crash, then the elder of the two will be deemed to have died first. So John's estate will pass totally to Mary, tax free because of the spouse exemption, but the whole estate of £500,000 will then pass to Mary's beneficiaries with only her nil rate band of £223,000, leaving £277,000 taxable at 40%, i.e. £110,800.

Had the wills been drafted with a survivorship clause, i.e. "I leave everything to Mary so long as she survives me by 30 days, and if not, to my kids, Jane and Jimmy", then what would have happened is that John's half of the estate would have passed on his death with Mary's passing on hers, each entitled to £223,000 exemption, and a final tax bill of only £21,600 being 40% on £54,000. A saving of £89,200 for one clause in a will!

The Use of Trusts

The word "Trust", confuses many people. But this is unnecessary. A trust is just a mechanism for holding property. The "Trustees" are the people who are responsible for property which is actually owned legally by the beneficiaries. For some reason, the creator of the trust (the settlor), does not want the beneficiaries to have immediate access to the funds.

This may be because they are children, or even because they are not yet born. It may be because they are irresponsible and could fritter away all the wealth. It could also be because a wealthy family wishes to protect their family line against golddiggers who marry into the family.

A trust can be very simple, such as a 'bare trust' where really the trustees are just acting as nominees holding assets for another specified person. That person can get at the assets whenever he or she wants to.

An 'interest in possession' trust is one where specified individuals are actually entitled to the income and possibly the capital of the fund. A 'discretionary trust' is one where no-one is actually entitled, but a variety of people may be entitled at the trustees discretion. Finally, an 'accumulation and maintenance' trust is a special type of discretionary trust for the benefit of children up to the age of 25. There are certain inheritance tax benefits and a different inheritance tax treatment for each of these trusts.

Why Use a Trust?

Many people see that they have an inheritance tax problem and want to give money away. However, they also see that the recipients of that money may not yet be ready for it, either because they are too young or rather irresponsible. However, the money can be put into a Trust so that from that point on, the individuals own it but they can't get at it.

So the money leaves the donor's estate for inheritance tax purposes and goes into the estate of the recipients, but the control of those funds remains with the people who created the Trust in the first place. This is very useful if grandparents wish to give money to their grandchildren. Section 1 shows how Trusts can be used to give complete freedom from income tax, capital gains tax and even inheritance tax.

The tax savings more generally associated with trusts would work as follows: Imagine you have a cash account which you would like ultimately to give to your children. At present, you don't really need it, but you don't want to release it to them just yet. What you might do is put the asset in a trust from which they can benefit at some time in the future. The actual gift into the trust would be likely to be free of inheritance tax so long as you survive it by seven years.

In the meantime, all the increase in the asset's value will fall out of your estate immediately. Seven years later all the money and all the growth are outside your estate having improved your inheritance tax position enormously, and yet, the children haven't yet got their hands on the money. This is perhaps the most common use of trusts for inheritance tax, and the amount saved is entirely dependant on the amount you put in there in the first place.

Loans For Trusts

Now, however, you face a problem. You've got rid of wealth from your estate but you find yourself in need of cash. Well, good news, your advisor drafted a trust with wide powers and one of them is to be able to lend you money. So, you simply ask the trustees (yourself and your spouse), they agree and you get your cash! It's rather more complex than this but it can be done.

You will need to be careful because the Government slipped a few proposals in the 1994 Finance Bill to tax such loans in certain circumstances. You will need expert advice to pick your way through the mine field.

Year End Tax Planning

£ This topic deserves a section in itself because it is at the end of the year that most people consider tax planning, and in many cases, such as Bed and Breakfasting, the timing of disposals or the repatriation of overseas funds, this can only be considered right at the end of the tax year. Here is a check list of things you might consider towards the end of the tax year:

❑ Make sure you have repatriated any funds if you have low income in the tax year.

❑ Make sure you have taken up your entitlement to ISA.

❑ Make sure you have paid your pension contributions and made any elections that are necessary. (See Section 7).

❑ Make sure you have used your capital gains tax annual exemption, through Bed and Breakfasting if necessary.

❑ Make sure you have used your inheritance tax annual exemptions, normal expenditure exemptions, or £250 gift allowances.

❑ Make sure you have discussed any National Insurance arrangements with your employer.

❑ Finally, make sure you have made any necessary elections to do with your tax affairs, particularly where time limits are involved.

Another important function of the end of tax year planning season is to use the impetus created to just do something. Most of the tax planning done in the last quarter of the financial year is not specific to the year end but people just focus on the 5th of April and do all the things they should have done earlier, like sorting out their wills or setting up the offshore trust.

But remember, your advisers are likely to be under pressure at this time of year and so, where possible, get your thoughts together over the summer when all concerned will have the time to consider all the implications surrounding your plan.

Happy Families
The Wisemanns

£ Granny Wisemann sat back in her comfortable leather arm chair and smiled. The television seemed to smile back at her. The stockmarket had risen again. It seemed that as each day went by, not only did she increase her own personal wealth, but the family trust she had created also grew in value. She had settled £100,000 eight years previously and now the value was twice that, and all free of tax. How many of her friends had held on to funds unnecessarily only for them to be depleted by the effects of inheritance tax?

"Why so smug?" Her son Rupert, being a salesman, was sensitive to people's moods.

"I.C.I." was granny's simple reply.

"Really?" continued Rupert glancing at the TV screen and never doubting for one moment the further inevitable increase in price since his mother had tipped the shares.

"They've doubled," he said, "that's me out."

Sensing his mother's interest, he continued. "Don't worry, there won't be any tax implications. Half of the shares are in my personal equity plan and the rest are in my pension scheme. In fact, I can't remember the last time I paid any tax at all on share dividends or share gains."

The cork of the champagne bottle popped noisily and hit the ceiling. But this was no occasional celebration. For Rupert Wisemann drank a bottle of champagne every week, bought with the National Insurance split he had negotiated with his employer some years earlier on his pension payments.

The relaxed tranquillity of the evening was suddenly interrupted. "It's not fair!" shouted a shrill voice, followed by heavy stamping up the ornate staircase of the large detached house. Whilst Rupert's daughter had shouted with all the frustration of a young teenager, it was most unlikely that the neighbours, separated by a three acre garden, could have heard her.

"Oh dear," said Rupert "it'll be that pony business again."
"Sorry?" asked granny, not understanding.
"Portia wants a pony". Granny looked surprised.
"Well, give her one Rupert, for goodness sake, what's 50 quid?"
"No granny, a real pony. An actual horse."

Granny looked pensive. "Look Rupert, let me buy a pony. I'm not using all my income and really it would probably fall under my normal expenditure exemption for inheritance tax."

"No mother, you've done enough," objected Rupert. "If she really wants one then we've got the accumulation and maintenance trust which Dad left. That's absolutely stuffed full of money, so I'm sure we could buy her one out of that."

Now that the discussion was firmly into personal finances, granny Wisemann wanted to continue, directing the strategy. "I was thinking of repatriating part of my off-shore roll-up fund. You know, perhaps to pay for the children's next holiday."

"But what about the tax mother?" asked Rupert immediately biting his tongue, knowing there would be an answer.

"No problem, I've just bought into an Enterprise Investment Scheme, so I won't pay any tax at all this year. I might as well repatriate the funds." Rupert sat back watching the beads in his crystal glass dance with the excited fizz of the duty free champagne. It was all so easy.

"You realise that if Portia gets a horse, Algernon will have to have a junior trials bike?" Granny Wisemann adjusted the electric lumbar support in her chair and tilted back to the pre-set reclining position she had abandoned to watch the evening news. A slight nod indicated that she understood, but that sums of £10,000 or less were no longer of any significance.

After a few moments of silence, Penelope Wisemann came through the double doors into the large sitting room, her elegant designer clothes and coiffure set off by the family trait, a broad smile. "How did you get on darling?" asked Rupert, knowing that his wife's appearance signified an enjoyable victory at the Bridge Club. "Well, apart from my partner making one or two rather stupid calls, we managed to win pretty convincingly."

Rupert had instinctively moved over to the drinks cabinet and taken out another champagne glass, "You'd better have a glass of this then darling."

"No thanks darling, I'll just have mineral water," replied Penelope thinking of her aerobics class and the fight she'd had to maintain her figure since it had become unnecessary for her to work any more.

"Who was your partner?" asked granny Wisemann. "It was Margo Sadleben whose husband works with Rupert. She really was off form." Granny Wisemann gave Rupert a knowing nod. "At times I could hardly play for laughing," continued Penelope, "You wouldn't believe some of the things that Margo was saying." Granny Wisemann`s chair buzzed into a more upright position, indicating that she would like to judge for herself.
"Margo's husband is a chartered accountant, it seems that their financial affairs are a disaster. He's lost his tax appeal over selling off part of the garden from their last house."

"Didn't know the system," muttered Rupert, almost as though it were an epitaph.

"One really does feel sorry for them," continued Penelope. "Her children never get to go on any of the school trips because they are always short of hard cash." Granny Wisemann's contemptuous cough indicated precisely how sympathetic she felt.

"I can't understand why they have no money," continued Penelope. "I mean, he drives such a big car."

"Yes," interjected Rupert, "one with a high 'list price', and with a two point one litre engine! Doesn't do his business miles either. I don't wonder that all his money goes on the tax."

"But he doesn't seem to have any luck," protested Penelope.
"Luck! You make your own luck where tax is concerned," snapped Rupert, repeating one of his mother's famous mottos. There was a lull in which Rupert continued to consider his colleague's plight.

"The last time I saw him it was actually rather embarrassing. I was in the VIP lounge at Heathrow and he wandered in. So, I bought him a drink and began to chat, when who should I meet but Stefan Bernstein. If ever there was an opportunity to make Henry Sadleben appreciate all the mistakes he's making, it would have been to spend the flight talking to the erudite Dr Bernstein. But you wouldn't believe what happened. As we went to board the plane, it turned out that Henry was in economy class!"

"And that's where people like him will stay!" interrupted granny Wisemann. "And if he doesn't brighten up his ideas, he'll be in with the luggage next time."
"Oh, you two are horrid," giggled Penelope. It was easy to find things funny in her position. She was a very wealthy woman in her own right, not just because the family's assets had always

been split in the most tax efficient manner, but through the various mechanisms that Dr Bernstein had recommended, she paid little or no tax.

The relaxed evening was interrupted by the appearance of the housekeeper. A dour looking Scots woman in her late fifties. Morag McGrabber was paid for by the money Rupert saved each year on his tax relievable enterprise zone investments.

"It's the carpet man madam," said Morag, delivering the line as though it were the final statement in a particularly uplifting moral stage drama.

"The carpet man?" enquired Rupert. "Yes darling," replied Penelope. "I thought I'd have the guest room re-carpeted, you know how you like to make people feel welcome."

"What's the damage then?" asked Rupert, smiling, realising there was no need to argue. "Well, how do I know?" replied Penelope. "I don't know what I want yet."

Rupert drained his glass and held it up to the crystal chandelier, watching the myriad reflections and sparkles making the glass appear as if it were still full. Within a couple of seconds, it was. "Oh come on Rupert, don't go quiet on me," began Penelope, "I mean, you can't take it with you."

"You're right," laughed Rupert, adding, "In that case, you might as well do our bedroom whilst you're at it!"

"And do the hall, stairs and landing too," said granny Wisemann. "It should be covered by my annual IHT allowance."

" I love tax planning," said Penelope finishing her mineral water and hurrying off excitedly to meet the carpet man.

The Sadlebens

"Why the face?" began Henry Sadleben. He was spoiling for a fight. "Lost at bridge again?"

Margo Sadleben put down her slightly shabby handbag and moved over to the drinks cabinet to pour herself a large cheap whisky, which they'd imported on a day trip to Calais. Henry held up his glass automatically. "Yes, you might as well Henry, this is the only tax you've ever saved."

Henry sighed heavily. He knew he had failed. Once, his family had been very wealthy, but high rates of income tax in the 70's had used up capital and death duties had all but depleted the estate to nothing when his parents died. He had a high gross income, but he seemed to pay so much tax. That damned car! Then there was his mother, dependant on the State and what little he could afford. Where had it all gone wrong?

"So, were you playing with Mr Veryclever's wife again?" Henry continued his attack. Margo didn't reply. Instead, she picked up her handbag and took out a letter. Holding it in front of Henry, she began, "It's from the Bursar of the school. He says that given our late payment of the fees for the last few terms, would we like to go and see him to talk about budgeting. Can you believe it! We must be the laughing stock of St. Vulcans." Henry sighed once again and drained his glass. The whisky seemed to attack his taste buds and always gave him a headache.

"The Wisemanns have a charitable educational trust and... "

"Shut up! I'm just about sick of the Wisemanns with their offshore bonds and their first class travel and their tax efficient company cars. 'Mester Wisemann esnae en, this is the hoos' kipper.' They think they're blinking royalty!" Margo shivered. It seemed rather cold in the old damp house without any heating on.

"Keep your voice down Henry, the neighbours will hear."

"Oh yes," replied Henry, "the precious blinking neighbours with their ears to the wall."

"Look Henry, we need to talk. We're down to our last few pounds in our Building Society account. Penelope says it should be in my name, as you probably pay 40% tax and -" she realised it was futile.

"Look, we'll sell the shares," continued Henry, "We'll just have to take the tax on the chin. If only Dad hadn't held over the gain, and had made a proper will. We'll be clobbered again. What with that overdraft because of the tax I've had to pay!"

Henry recalled Rupert telling him that the official rate of interest was only a quarter of that on his overdraft. And there was no tax relief on the loan! Henry felt tired and ill. If he hadn't had to cancel his BUPA subscription, he would probably have had a check up. But £700 was just too much at the moment. How did Rupert get it for £90? And how did Rupert manage to sell a plot of land without paying any capital gains tax? Everything just seemed to be conspiring against Henry.

Through the side of his empty glass Henry looked over at Margo. Her hair was moving very slightly, as it always did. There was a nervousness that meant she was never still. She had been out playing bridge when Henry had arrived home and this was the first conversation they'd had.

"You might as well know now," continued Henry, seeing no reason to suppress the information, "I've been made redundant. Don't worry, I'll be getting a payoff, but it won't be much after tax."

"Didn't Rupert Wisemann get £30,000 tax free when he was made redundant before be joined your firm?" asked Penelope, wishing she had bitten her tongue.

Henry stood up and took a deep breath. Suddenly, in his wife's eyes, he had a resolve which had been missing in him for years. "What time is it Margo?" he asked.

"Eight thirty," was his wife's uncomfortable and mystified reply. "Right, I can still get there."

"Where Henry?" asked Margo, fearing a drinking binge at the Golf Club that they could ill afford.

"The library."
"The library?"
"Yes, it's open until nine, and there's still time to get there."
"Whatever for?" asked Margo.
"I think it's about time I went and got that blinking Bernstein book!"

"I'll drink to that!" said Margo.

Past Legal Cases Involving Taxation

Introduction

£ Over the years there have been a great many tax cases which have enhanced our understanding of how the law will be applied in particular circumstances.

Many are amusing, centring for example on whether a Jaffa Cake is in fact a biscuit or a cake. Other cases are far more useful, and often just as amusing. *This section gives you an important selection of those cases where the principles which have been decided could be of consequence to you in your own tax planning.* They will also be an almost endless source of after-dinner stories with which to bore your friends.

They think it's all over --- it is now.

After the 1966 World Cup, the late Bobby Moore received two particular payments. One was paid to him by a company as a prize for having won its 'Player of the Tournament' competition. The other was a bonus paid by the F.A. on the grounds that the team had won. What became the issue, was whether or not these payments were taxable under Schedule E as payments from his employment.

The High Court held that they were not taxable under Schedule E because they were not for any services which he had rendered. The point is that a payment to an employee has to be for some sort of services rendered, and it must therefore be within the scope of his ordinary duties. Whilst playing football was part of

Bobby Moore's duties, it was not necessarily contractual upon him to win!

They had to hand it to Shilton

In the late 1980s it was necessary for Nottingham Forest to sell the international goalkeeper, Peter Shilton. As part of the deal, Forest agreed to pay him £75,000 to encourage him to move. The Appeal Commissioners decided that this payment was an emolument of his employment, and therefore taxable.

The point was, whether the inducement payment from Nottingham Forest was a taxable emolument of Shilton's employment with his new club. If it were, then it would be assessable under Schedule E. The High Court, however, decided that the payment was not an emolument because it did not come directly from his employment with Southampton. That meant the payment could only be taxed as a golden handshake on which the taxation was markedly different.

Ground for Appeal

In 1980, Burnley Football Club went to the High Court over the cost of one of their stands. It had been deemed unsafe and was demolished, necessitating a new stand. The problem centred on whether the expenditure was revenue, i.e. something that you spend as you go along in running your business, or capital (a major one-off type of expenditure). The High Court ruled that the cost was capital and not revenue, which affected the speed of the tax write-off.

Not so glad all over

In the case of Read v Clark (1985), the taxpayer had been part of the Dave Clark Five. After the group broke up, he retained the copyright to many recordings, and later sold them to a foreign company for half a million dollars. He received the money whilst he was absent from the U.K. in the tax year 1978/79.

The issue centred on whether the taxpayer was still resident in the U.K. because that was his usual residence, and therefore only overseas for a temporary purpose.

The Court decided that the absence had constituted non-residence and so the entire payment escaped tax.

Oh! Danny Boy

In 1926, the Old Bushmills Distillery took on the Revenue. They had gone into liquidation in 1920, and the liquidator had sold the stock. The company was assessed for the years 1920/21 and 1921/22 on the grounds that the liquidator was still trading.

The Recorder of Belfast disallowed the assessments, but the Revenue appealed because only one year had actually been over-ruled. The problem was, would this then apply to the second year? The Revenue won this one and perhaps the taxpayer drowned his sorrows.

Brandy Snapshot

Over fifty years ago, three independent wine traders bought some South African brandy and then shipped it to the U.K. blending it with its French equivalent. It was then sold in smaller quantities to new purchasers.

The point at issue was whether or not this constituted trading or was just a one-off transaction. The Court of Appeal decided that it was trading.

This is a very important case for anyone intending to carry out one, or a series of, transactions which in themselves might not appear to be a trade. For example, in the case of Martin v Lowry (1926), a large quantity of linen was bought from the Government by a farmer with no previous interest in the linen business. He set up a firm to sell the linen, and in fact did so to a variety of purchasers. The House of Lords held that he was trading and his profits were therefore assessable under Schedule D.

This case could have important repercussions for people who perhaps sell a few motor vehicles, or their own paintings. But this can work both ways. Once you are assessed to trading you will be able to benefit from the various trading deductions, and you might even post a loss. So don't panic if you are assessed to trading because it might be to your advantage. Simply make sure that you are ahead of the game by taking advice.

N.B. If you are trading speculatively in shares, you might well wish to be assessed as a trader, so that any losses you make are relievable. But following Salt v Chamberlain (1979), the rule is that anyone making speculative trades in securities will not be assessed as a trader.

Dual Purpose Underwear

There is an important principle for the self-employed. This says that if an individual is spending money on an item 'wholly and exclusively for business use', then that item will be tax deductible. For example, if one takes professional indemnity insurance, it has no other benefit than allowing you to trade.

Other expenditure may not be so clear cut. In the case of Mallalieu v Drummond (1983), a practising lady barrister was obliged to buy black dresses and clothing. She tried to claim the cost of this against taxation. The House of Lords reversed the decision of both the High Court and the Court of Appeal.

Their Lordships decided that the expenditure was not wholly and exclusively incurred for the lady's profession as a barrister, because there was a dual purpose of preserving warmth and decency by wearing clothing in the first place.

This further motive therefore prevented the expenditure from being deductible. So, if you are claiming an expense it will need to conform to the 'wholly and exclusively' test.

No each-way Bet

In the case of Sharkey v Werner (1955), the wife of the taxpayer had a business of breeding horses on a stud farm, but she also ran a racing stable. It was agreed that the racing stable was not a trade. Many of the horses which had been bred at the stud farm were transferred to the racing stable and the accounts always indicated that the horses were transferred at the cost of their breeding. The tax man argued that the market value of the horses would be the right amount to take into account for the purposes of tax.

The principle on which this case rests is the value of trading stock removed from a business. (You can make the analogy of the grocer who walks into the shop and grabs a handful of carrots).

The House of Lords agreed that it was the market value of the horses that must be used for tax purposes rather than their costs. How many grocers, however, keep a strict record of the bags of carrots they eat is anyone's guess!

Went to a Garden Varty

In the case of Varty v Lynes (1976), the taxpayer had a house with a garden. He sold the house and part of the garden and was free of capital gains tax because it was his private residence. But a year later, after having got planning permission, he sold the rest of the garden for a substantial profit.

The High Court decided that the disposal of the rest of the garden did not qualify under the private residence exemption, and capital gains tax had to be paid. The important principle here is that if you are intending to do this, you should sell your garden first and then sell the rest of your house, because at the time you sold the garden, it will be part of your house, and may therefore qualify for exemption. Selling it afterwards just won't work.

It is worth looking at the case of Makins v Elson in the same year. The taxpayer bought some land on which to build a house. Whilst doing so he lived in a caravan, which was connected to mains services. He sold the whole site before finishing the job, including the caravan, and was assessed to capital gains tax.

The question was, did the sale of the caravan fall within the ordinary private residence exemption, and the High Court decided that it did. So, even if you lived in a temporary caravan, you can sometimes avoid capital gains, although if you are clever enough to make a capital gain on a caravan, you probably don't need tax advice.

But the taxpayer in Markey v Sanders (1987) did need advice. He owned a small country estate of some twelve acres, and also a three bedroomed bungalow in its own garden at the end of a long drive. When he sold the whole estate, he hoped that the bungalow and the main house would all count as one single house for the purpose of his CGT exemption.

Unfortunately, the High Court disagreed on the grounds that the bungalow itself did not enhance the enjoyment of the main house, and was not sufficiently close to it to form part of a single block of buildings. Williams v Merrylees (1987) had a more successful result for the taxpayer who managed to sell his four acre estate along with his house and a separate lodge, because it was held by the High Court that the lodge formed part of the overall residence.

The message is clear, if you are approaching the sale of a substantial property, take advice first.

The Duke of Hazzard

The Duke of Westminster put in place deeds of covenant for some employees. These employees could either have thrown in their jobs and still have been entitled to the payments, or remained in office and claimed their salaries as well. If fact, all they got was a covenanted payment.

The problem was whether the payments to the employees should be treated as covenants, which was their legal form, or whether they were really disguised wages.

The House of Lords decided that it was not within their power to disregard the legal effect of a properly drafted document. The payments were covenants and had to be taxed accordingly.

This established a vital principle. Unless a document is a complete sham, the Court cannot disregard its legal consequences, however inconvenient. Lord Normand later commented "Tax avoidance is an evil, but it will be the beginning of a much greater evil if the Courts were to over-stretch .... in order to subject a taxation to people of whom they disapproved".

Unfortunately, since the 1930s, things have changed considerably!

Ring-a Ring-a Roses

There are two very complex cases mentioned in our tax avoidance section, namely, the case of Ramsay (1981) and the later case of Furniss v Dawson. Both these cases centred on slightly artificial schemes which had a variety of steps within them. The point at stake was whether or not the Court should look at each step independently, or the overall effect.

The basic decision of the House of Lords was that steps which are inserted into a pre-agreed series of transactions for no other reason than to avoid tax, can be disregarded. This means that the tax consequences revert to those which would have been the case, if a series of transactions had not included the particular steps in question.

These two cases have done more to clarify and tighten up the law on complicated avoidance schemes than any others.

What cards have you got?

In 1986, Rothschild Holdings had telephone confirmation concerning Revenue practice on Stamp Duty. Subsequently, the tax man disagreed and Rothschilds sought an order for discovery of the Revenue's internal papers to see whether or not the practice in question existed. The Court of Appeal upheld the decision of the High Court and allowed a Discovery Order. This was the first time in which this had been allowed against the Inland Revenue and was therefore a most significant victory for the taxpayer.

Don't bank on it

As long ago as 1892, the agent of a bank was asked by his employer to live at the bank which had accommodation specifically for this reason. The point was whether or not the value of this accommodation was part of the agent's income.

The House of Lords held that the value of the house was not an emolument of the agent, establishing the principle that in order to be taxable in the hands of an employee, a benefit must be capable of conversion into cash. Before you start to get too excited, you will note that in the last century this principle has been rather updated by specific legislation on benefits!

An Englishman's Home

A taxpayer had the costs of keeping his home in good order paid by a company of which he was a director and controlling shareholder. The question was whether or not the fact that the company discharged his liabilities in this regard would constitute assessable income. The High Court decided that it did because the payment of the bills constituted 'monies worth', and following the principle in the case above, was assessable.

First Impressions...

In the case of Scorer v Olin (1985), the taxpayer claimed certain loss reliefs and the Inspector agreed them by mistake. Some years later, another Inspector spotted the error and tried to raise additional assessments for the people in question.

The key issue was whether or not the second Inspector was entitled to discover the error and then raise new assessments, or whether the taxpayer was protected by the previous Inspector's mistakes. The House of Lords decided the taxpayer was safe, and the original Inspector's agreement stood.

Very Illuminations

In 1988 the Blackpool Marton Rotary Club received interest from its deposit account, but didn't submit tax returns. The tax man assessed the club to corporation tax on the grounds that it was an unincorporated association, and therefore a company for tax purposes.

The question at stake was whether or not the club was a partnership and therefore liable to income tax and perhaps personal allowances, or whether it was a corporation. The High Court held that it was correctly assessed to corporation tax and the tax was chargeable.

Several cans of heavy

Scottish and Newcastle Breweries spent over £100,000 on lighting and decoration in their premises in order to attract up-market clients. The question was whether or not this was 'plant' and therefore whether it would qualify for capital allowances.(Special deductions against tax.) The House of Lords agreed that it was plant and therefore qualified for the deduction. If you have always thought of plant as a JCB rather than a mural of a bull-fighter and sad-eyed spanish girl, perhaps you should drink more of the Scottish and Newcastle Breweries products.

(Whether Wimpy's failure to have the lighting in Pizza Land allowed as plant in 1989 is anything to do with their Lordships' preference for Newcastle Brown rather than parmesan cheese is anyone's guess.)

The cheque is in the post

In the case of Owen (1949), a taxpayer gave money to three relatives. Even though he drew the cheques and gave them to the relatives three years before he died, they were not actually credited to the relatives' bank accounts until a date which fell within the three year period before the taxpayer's death. The question at stake was when the gift had taken place, was it when he gave the cheques or when they were cleared?

The High Court decided that the gift was paid within the three years and was thus liable to tax. The principle here is that the time of a gift made by cheque is when it is credited to the recipient's bank account, and not when it is drawn by the payer. This is therefore a vital case whenever a deadline is involved.

Stupid Boy

In the 1981 case of Bentley v Pike, the taxpayer's wife inherited property in Germany. This was in 1967, although it was not for five years that she was entered in the German Land Registry. In 1973 the property had been sold and the proceeds received in Deutschmarks.

The problem was twofold. What was the actual date of acquisition, (was it her father's death in 1967, or the date that she was entered in the Land Register?). Secondly, was the amount of the gain to be assessed in Deutschmarks and then converted to Sterling, or simply calculated in Sterling all along?

The High Court decided that the gain must be assessed entirely in Sterling, taking no account of any exchange gains or losses. Secondly, the date of acquisition was that of the father's death, irrespective of when the property was registered.

Another case involving the Germans was one in which a taxpayer got a job overseas with a German publishing firm and his wife transferred a farm to his ownership. Once he left for Germany, he sold the farm by auction with the Revenue assessing some £60,000 of capital gains tax.

However, there is a special concession that allows you to be treated as non-resident from the day you leave the country, and the taxpayer depended on this to escape the tax. This went all the way to the High Court where it was decided that the Revenue provided concessions to help people and that they need not allow them to be abused for tax avoidance. The Revenue were not, therefore, forced to apply a concession, and the taxpayer failed.

Chartered Stupidity

A taxpayer had a business developing property, and had accountants to handle the tax matters. The accountants produced
accounts which had failed to show private expenditure and also
indicated the taxpayer to be in partnership when he wasn't.
The Revenue wanted to raise further assessments many years
later, and had to prove wilful default in order to do so.

The High Court decided that the tax payer was innocent of wilful
default since he had listened to the advice of his accountants.
However, the accountants were guilty of wilful default on the cli-
ent's behalf! The further tax assessments were therefore valid
and interest and tax had to be paid.

This demonstrates that your accountants had better be good, or
they can land you in it.

In another case, a barrister was served with a notice meaning he
had to produce documents relevant to the taxman's case. However, the barrister refused and the Revenue sought to prosecute
him. The points was whether the documents were the subject of
legal professional privilege. If they were, then the barrister could
not have made them available. In the High Court, the barrister
won and did not need to show the documents.

I had that Bernstein in the back of the cab once

In the leading case of Calvert v Wainwright, it was held that a taxi
driver's tips were taxable. This is because they flow so directly
from the business he is in. It is this case that has allowed the
Inland Revenue to assess a great many individuals who habitually
receive tips, such as taxi drivers, waiters, doormen and so on.
So the next time you give a taxi driver a cash tip, you can be certain he will be putting it on his tax return.

Very strict Madam!

In another leading case, the judge was not submissive, and held
that even though profits might be gained from an illegal activity,

they are still taxable, irrespective of that activity. For example, gambling winnings by those who gamble regularly for a living, will be taxable, as are the earnings of prostitutes and other less well recognised entertainers. Unfortunately, tipping a prostitute for particularly good service out of your gambling winnings will not be an allowable deduction!

Pass the Port

If you need evidence that the Customs and Excise, who administer VAT, are more serious than the taxman, then this is a case in point. In CCE v Lord Fisher, Customs and Excise raised VAT assessments on the Lord, because he was running regular shoots on his property and obtained substantial contributions from those who joined him. He made his own contribution as well, but this cut no ice with the VAT man.

Thankfully the High Court decided that this was not a business and that activities carried on for social enjoyment do not constitute a taxable supply for VAT.

Thirty pieces of silver + VAT

The Church of Scientology of California had a UK business whereby it promoted its religious faith. Customs and Excise assessed it on the grounds that it was a business making taxable supplies.

The point at issue was whether or not the furtherance of a religion actually constituted running a business. The Court of Appeal decided that there was in fact no legal reason why a body promoting its religious views could not be construed as carrying on a business for the purposes of a VAT assessment. So there is VAT on your beliefs!

Ghost VAT men in the sky

In 1988 British Airways Plc fought an assessment to VAT on the grounds that the food they provided in flight was a second supply

---

over and above the supply of air travel. The Court ruled that there was just the one supply of air travel, and that the catering was merely incidental. So, next time you eat a rubber trifle, you can smile to yourself and the fact that you have beaten the VAT man will make it all the more tasty.

A little knowledge...

You might think that if you had no knowledge whatsoever of the VAT system, nor its application to you, that there would be some relief if you broke one of the rules. Unfortunately, the case of Neal v Customs and Excise 1988 gives little hope. In the case in question the individual should have notified the VAT man of a liability to register, but of course failed to do so as he had no idea that she was supposed to.

The Courts debated the issue of whether ignorance of law was a reasonable excuse for the taxpayer not having notified the VAT man. Unfortunately the High Court decided that ignorance of the law is not a good enough excuse. So go back to the beginning of this book and read it again!

And Finally...

This is only a small selection of the tax cases which could have been included. As you can see, a great many individuals, even those with professional advice, have fallen foul of the taxman one way or another.

This is what makes this book so valuable. Rather than asking you to become involved in wild schemes or untried strategies, the book sets out a great many well trodden paths to success. One thing is for certain, you will never see the case of Bernstein v The Inland Revenue!

Conclusion

So now you have read how the rich and famous manage to stay rich and famous, how loopholes may be exploited that save anything from a few pounds to tens of thousands of pounds a year, how individuals can benefit, how a husband and wife can benefit, how the family unit can benefit and how one generation after another can continue to hold the same wealth without seeing it diminish by a series of tax charges.

Without ever breaking the law, you can make it work for you and improve you lifestyle, not only by enhancing your capital base, the wealth you actually own, but by improving your income flow. How many readers of this book would argue all day for a slightly bigger pay rise, when if they directed their energies towards tax saving, they could increase their net spendable income much more significantly than any 5% pay rise.

But whilst this book has demonstrated the massive scope for saving significant sums of tax, you must remember the golden rules.

1.   Learn how to use the tax system and the officials within it.

2.   Make sure you have all your facts together and that you have done a reasonable amount of research.

3.   Make sure you get all your allowances first and foremost.

4.   Make sure you have as much that is tax free, both in terms of income and capital taxes, as is practical.

5.   Always look at the net return to you as an individual and don't let the tail wag the dog.

---

6. Don't allow yourself to get involved in overcomplicated schemes of your own conception, bearing in mind the cases of Furniss v Dawson and Ramsay.

7. Always bear in mind your executors and beneficiaries, if you effect any wild and wacky tax arrangements which may only come to light after your death.

Good Luck!

Stefan Bernstein

Using The Taxman

Can you imagine if you had never heard of the game of Chess, had no idea how the pieces moved or what the rules were? If you then sat down with someone who played every day, how long do you think you would last? Of course, you would never do this. And yet, so may people take on the full time tax professionals at the Inland Revenue without ever understanding the rules. And guess what? They lose.

You can make far more rapid progress to a resolution of your affairs and thereby reach a point where you can plan more effectively, if you know how to use the system. There are several basic rules you should be aware of:

1)   Be prepared - have your tax reference and National Insurance number if you are telephoning the Inland Revenue, so that you will be able to speak to the right person.

2)   Always ask for a name, so that you can continue your dialogue with that same person.

3)   If you are talking about allowances, pensions, or general issues, ask for the Allocation Officer.

4)   If your query concerns corporation tax, capital allowances or self-employed issues, ask for an Inspector.

5)   Remember, you should always be dealt with immediately if you telephone.

6)   If you write to the Inland Revenue, their policy statement says that they will deal with over 90% of the post they

receive within 28 days. So, if you get no response, contact the management Inspector and ask why not.

7)   If you are not satisfied, work up the chain below.

REGIONAL CONTROLLER

DISTRICT INSPECTOR

MANAGEMENT INSPECTOR   TECHNICAL INSPECTOR

ALLOCATION OFFICER

8)   Have a look at the extract from the Taxpayers' Charter at the end of this book. The Inland Revenue is supposed to be there to help you and you will find that a lot of the difficult work, such as the calculation of carried forward pension relief, may be done for you.

The tax Inspector may often threaten you with "The General Commissioners". This is in fact, a body of impartial people and they will adjudicate on any dispute. This may well work in your favour.

Of course, to get the best from this tactic, you will need to turn up to any hearing to put your case across. In general, if you do turn up, the Commissioner will be sympathetic, but as they deal with many hundreds of cases, your failure to turn up will leave them with only one side of the argument and you will be in a far weaker position.

So, do your preparation, understand the system, and use it.

Remember - using the system is half the battle.

Law and Principles

Normally, the law on tax is clear cut. For example, there is no way you can deduct the cost of a new three piece suite for your living room simply because you sit there after a hard day at the office. However, if you are self employed you can deduct the cost of the petrol you use directly on the business, for example, visiting customers, or prospective customers.

Where things get difficult is on the margins of the law. For example, certain businesses are able to deduct the costs of overalls or protective clothing for the purposes of their tax computations. But a recent case ruled that a lady barrister, forced to wear black clothing as part of Court etiquette, could not actually deduct the cost of that clothing from her tax assessment. Here was a barrister taking a case to the Inland Revenue and losing. It is on this question of interpreting the law where most problems arise.

In the first instance, you will probably disagree with an Inspector who is trying to apply the law and the Inland Revenue's interpretation of it in a way with which you disagree. If you are not happy, then you may go to the Commissioners for independent arbitration. After that, you go to law, that is to say, you take your case to Court.

This process is important and you should understand it, because it amplifies the law and gives you precedent, that is to say it establishes what the law really means. There is a whole body of tax cases, which,

---

like the case of the lady barrister, have clarified and amplified the law. For example, the case of Shilton v Wilmshurst, involved the former England International goalkeeper and clarified certain points on Golden Handshakes. The point is this - if you do your preparation thoroughly and use the system early on, you may avoid becoming an expensive "tax case" for students to quote in the future. Read the section on tax laws. It will probably amuse you but at the same time will help you to understand how the system works and how relatively small distinctions or nuances of meaning can result in success or failure.

Anti Avoidance

A very important principle the amateur tax planner must understand is that of anti-avoidance. Over the years, once a loophole is highlighted, quite understandably, the Inland Revenue will try to close it by introducing anti-avoidance legislation or by applying the principle from another tax case.

There are two major cases in this regard known as Furniss v Dawson and Ramsay v CIR. Broadly speaking, these two cases established the principle that if the sole motive for a complicated set of transactions is to avoid tax, then the law will look at the reality of the transactions and tax them accordingly. *This is fundamental and you must understand it.*

For example, if you give your children money, then the interest arising on it will normally be taxed on you.

However, you might agree to give your neighbour's children £50,000 and for your neighbour to give your children £50,000. In that case, you would not have given your children any money and so the interest they gain on the £50,000 should be their own tax free interest.

However, the principles of these two tax cases would operate to outlaw the scheme on the grounds of the reality being that both you and your neighbour had effectively given your own children money. Please keep this concept in mind in all your dealings with the Taxman.

Taxation Of Investments

Building Societies Bank Deposits	Basic and higher rate income tax may be due but no capital gains tax. Basic rate tax usually deducted at source.
National Savings Bank Ordinary A/C	First £70 per annum of interest is tax free above that basic and higher rate tax may be due, but no tax is deducted at source. No C.G.T.
National Savings Income Bonds	Basic and higher rate tax may be due but no C.G.T. Tax not deducted at source.
Guaranteed Income Bonds	No basic rate tax to pay but possible higher rate tax due after basic rate credit. No C.G.T.
Gilts	Basic and higher rate tax may be due on income element. Some gilts paid gross if purchased via post office. No C.G.T.
National Savings Certs	Tax free if held for requisite period.

Shares Unit/Investment Trusts	Dividends liable to both basic and higher rates of income tax and basic rate is deducted at source. C.G.T. also may be due.
Debentures/loan stock	Basic and higher rate tax may be due, basic rate deducted at source. No C.G.T.
Insurance Bonds (onshore)	No basic rate tax liability but higher rate (less basic rate) may be due on profit element. No C.G.T.
Personal Equity Plans /ISA	No tax due.
Pensions	Basic and higher rate may be due on pension income, tax relief due on way in.
Offshore Roll-Up Fund	No tax due until fund is encashed.
Purchased Life Annuities	Basic and higher rate tax may be due but only on a proportion

Appendix Four

How Much Can You Save?

The list below is intended to summarise the approximate amounts that you can saved by proper tax planning. The appropriate section will explain how to do it in detail.

HOW?	HOW MUCH? £
Personal Equity Plan	250 p.a.
Mortgage Capital Relief	275 p.a.
Gifts on Marriage	400-2000
£250 gifts	100 p.a.
Annual gifts	1,200 p.a.
Children's Allowances	1,678 p.a.
Widows' Bereavement Allowance	570 (for two years)
Bed and Breakfast/spouse	2,320
Loss timing	2,720
Disposal timing	1,000

HOW?	HOW MUCH? £
National Insurance	10.0% of salary
Independent Taxation	6,414 (Income Tax)
" "	2,720 (C.G.T.)
Pension Contributions	7% of income
Redundancy/Severance	12,000
Deed of Variation	89,200
Will's survivorship clause	89,200
Self managed pension	96,000
Earnings Cap	Unlimited
Offshore Bond	Unlimited
P.E.Ts.	Unlimited
Trusts	Unlimited
Generation skipping	Unlimited

GLOSSARY

Age Allowance

An increased personal allowance for those people aged over 65 at the beginning of the tax year.

Anti-Avoidance

Specific legislation introduced by the Inland Revenue to combat avoidance schemes.

Avoidance

The use of legitimate means to reduce ones tax bill.

Bed and Breakfast

A system of selling and immediately reacquiring assets in order to realise a chargeable gain, or allowable loss.

Business Expansion Scheme

An investment on which full tax relief is available on subscription and the proceeds of which are entirely free after a five year qualifying period.

Benefits in Kind/ Fringe Benefits

Benefits provided by an employer for which the employee does not usually have to pay. For example, company cars or company accommodation.

Commissioners

Either special Commissioners who are full time professionals, or general Commissioners who are unpaid local people. Each is intended to adjudicate where there is a dispute between the taxpayer and the Inland Revenue.

Chargeable Gains (allowable losses)	When a chargeable asset is sold, there will either be a profit or a loss.
Deed of Variation	A mechanism by which a deceased person's will may be altered, usually to gain a tax advantage.
Domicile	The country you regard as your normal home.
Earnings Cap	A level of earnings beyond which pension contributions cannot be relieved.
Evasion	The use of illegal methods to avoid paying tax.
Estate	The total of an individual's property worldwide.
Furniss v Dawson	A fundamental tax case which sets out the Inland Revenue outlook on certain types of complicated tax avoidance schemes.
Gifts with Reservation	Gifts made to avoid inheritance tax, but which fail to do so because a benefit is reserved for the donor.
Intestate	A description whereby an individual has died without making a will, so that certain fall back provisions apply.
Interest in Possession	An individual's entitlement to the income of a trust.
Indexation Allowance	A means of allowing for inflation on chargeable gains.

Independent Taxation	A system whereby a husband and wife can be treated as entirely separate individuals for income tax purposes, and C.G.T.
ISA	Introduced in April 1999, an Individual Savings Account replaced PEPs and TESSAs
Ordinary Residence	Refers to your status as a taxpayer in the country in which you ordinarily live.
Personal Equity Plan (PEP)	A mechanism for the holding of shares or unit trusts on which there will be no income tax or capital gains tax.
PotentiallyExempt Transfer (PET)	Gifts between individuals and to certain trusts which will not become chargeable to inheritance tax unless the individual donor should die within seven years.
Personal Allowances	A set level of deduction from income before income tax is applied.
Residence	A term used specifically in taxation to denote an individual's temporary home for the purposes of taxation.
Roll-Up Fund	An offshore based investment where the interest content is accumulated year on year, without crystallising your tax liability until sold.
Spouse Exemption	This refers to the facility of passing unlimited assets between UK domiciled spouses without inheritance tax charges.

Taper Relief	A system whereby the inheritance tax charged on chargeable transfers is reduced to reflect the number of years since that transfer between three and seven. Or a system whereby CGT is reduced on assets based on how long they have been held.
TESSA	The Tax Exempt Special Savings arrangement, whereby the income from a deposit account may be credited without income tax deductions, subject to a five year holding period.
Trust	A mechanism where one party (the Trustee), hold assets for another party (the Beneficiaries), usually at the request of the Settlor (the one who introduced the assets in the first place).
Tax Payers Charter	A statement of Revenue policy as to how they will deal with the public.
Widows' Bereavement Allowance	A specific allowance which may be claimed by a widow in the year of her husband's death and the following year.
Year of Assessment	The tax year which runs from April 6th through to April 5th.

Benefits In Kind - Taxation Treatment

Benefits in Kind are taxed differently depending on the status of the recipient. Where the recipient is employed at a rate exceeding £8,500 per annum inclusive of the benefit charge, or where the individual is a director or an associate of a director as defined, then the charge to benefits is usually rather greater than for those individuals who are known as "non P11D employees".

The table below summarises the position.

Details	P11D Employee /Director	Non P11D Employee
Use of Company Assets	Taxable.	Normally not taxable
Private Use Motor Car	Taxable.	Generally tax free
Use of Company accommodation Rent free	Taxed on "Annual Value" except in cases where the employee must live there to perform his duties.	Taxed on "annual value" of benefit unless necessary to live there to form duties effectively.
Lunch Vouchers	Tax free up to 15p per day.	Tax free up to 15p per day.

Private Health Insurance Cover	Taxed on the amount of premium paid by the employee.	Tax free
Staff Canteen	Tax free provided the facilities are available to all members of staff.	Tax free
Interest Free Loan	Taxable generally.	Tax free
Credit Cards and Season Tickets	Taxable.	Taxable
Mobile telephones private use	Tax on £200 p.a.	Tax free

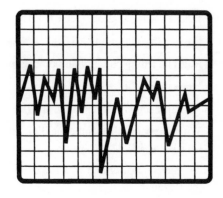

Further Information

The Inland Revenue publish a variety of useful leaflets and reportlets. Here is a list of the most important.

Leaflet	Topic
I.R. (Insert)	Shows all tax rates and allowances for current year. (see also I.R.90)
I.R. 34	This covers P.A.Y.E. (see I.R.69)
I.R. 58	This covers working abroad.
I.R. 60	This covers income tax and students.
I.R. 91	Allowances for widows.
I.R. 121	Income tax and pensioners.
I.R. 92	One parent families.
I.R. 93	Separation, divorce, maintenance.
I.R. 78	Personal pensions and Serps.
I.R. 89	P.E.P.S.
I.R. 110	Savings and investment. (see also I.R. 127)
I.R. 123	Mortgage relief.
I.R. 83	Independent Taxation. (see CGT 15)
C.G.T. 14	Basic introduction to C.G.T.
C.G.T. 4	Rules on letting part of your home. (see also I.R.87)
C.G.T. 13	Indexation relief.
I.M.T. 3	An introduction to inheritance tax. (see also I.H.T.1)
I.R. 45	What happens when someone dies with income tax, C.G.T. and I.H.T.
I.R. 120	Tax payers charter and how to get information from the Revenue.
I.R. 37	How to appeal against the decisions reached by the Revenue.

Understand Bonds & Gilts in a Day

This handy title shows potential investors, and those with an interest in the bond markets, how to assess the potential risks and rewards, giving a simple to follow set of criteria on which to base investment decisions. Having shown the inexperienced investor how to go about buying bonds, it also teaches even the most arithmetically shy how to calculate the yield on a bond and plan an income based portfolio. The confusing terminology used in the bond market is clearly explained with working definitions of many terms and a comprehensive glossary. **£6.95**

Understand Shares in a Day

Shows how the share market really works. Inexperienced investors will learn: ❏ About different types of shares ... ❏ Why share prices fluctuate... ❏ How to read the financial pages ... ❏ How shares are bought and sold ... ❏ How risk can be spread with investment and unit trusts ...❏ How to build a portfolio of shares ...❏ The risks and rewards associated with Penny Shares

Once this basic groundwork has been covered, the book explores more complex ideas which will appeal to both beginners and more experienced investors alike, including: ● How to value shares ● How equity options are used by professional investors to 'gear' profits and hedge against falling share prices. **£6.95**

£5.95

The Complete Beginner's Guide to The Internet

Everywhere you turn these days, it's Internet this, Cyberspace that and Superhighway the other. Indeed, hardly a day goes by without us being bombarded with information and reasons why you should be on the Net. But none of that is of much help in making an informed decision about joining and using the Internet.

What exactly is The Internet? Where did it come from and where is it going? And, more importantly, how can everybody take their place in this new community?

The Complete Beginner's Guide to The Internet answers all of those questions and more. On top of being an indispensable guide to the basics of Cyberspace, it is the lowest priced introduction on the market by a long way.

Tax Self-Assessment Made Easy
by Stefan Bernstein

The book tells you what you have to do and when to do it, warning you of what happens if you don't. Chapters include:
● Self-employed and the effects... ● Directors and trustees... ● Record keeping requirements
● Penalties and surcharges... ● People on PAYE ... ● What companies need to do... etc...

A valuable glossary and a variety of concise appendices make this book the complete and essential guide with schedules to help you ensure that your tax bill is correct in the first place.

£6.95

Timing The Financial Markets: Charting Your Way to Profit

Timing The Financial Markets shows all levels of investors, step-by-step, how to construct charts and graphs of price movements for bonds, shares and commodities. Then it explains, in easy-to-understand language, how to interpret the results and turn them into profit. **£6.95**